Top Questions from Real Interviews

In this section we're going to go into full detail about the thing that is on every job candidate's mind: what questions will I be asked, and how do I answer them? Not only will we tell you the answers to these questions, but we'll also go deep and get into what the interviewer is really asking and what they want to know.

The knowledge in this section comes from incredible experience- many years and hundreds of interviews from both sides of the interview table, so you'll get a complete perspective of each question. If you pay attention and absorb the concepts in this section, you'll undoubtedly do well in the most critical part of finding a new job and land a role you'll really love. Let's get down to business.

This section is organized very simply. We have a section for each question, and in each section we'll break down the most important information you need to understand: who will ask the question, what they're really asking, and what they really want to know. Remember that interview questions are almost always a little more than what's on the surface.

For example, do you think that when a hiring manager asks, "Tell me about yourself", that they want to know that you like to work out several days a week and occasionally watch HBO? Definitely not. There's more than meets the eye in that question, and others. Let the information in this section be the secret key that unlocks a true understanding of what interviewers want to know, and how you can actually connect with them and show you're a good fit.

What you need to do is read this chapter carefully and take notes. If anything is surprising or counterintuitive, make a note of it. Also, don't forget to read the last section, where we'll get into how you prepare and really maximize your effectiveness- because it's really not enough to just know what questions are going to be asked. Let's dive in.

Tell me about yourself

This question will likely come from a hiring manager, but can also be asked by a recruiter. You'll get asked this earlier in the interview process (typically during phone interviews).

What they're really asking

This question is definitely asking about your work, but more about how you got to where you are, rather than details about your current role. They're asking you to give a miniature version of your life story, but focused more on your work and career. If you're interviewing for your first role out of college, it should still be focused on what you've done to get yourself ready for a great career.

Note that they're not asking you to talk about your hobbies, what you do on weekends, your family, or your pet snake. Sometimes interviewers do want to get to know you a little bit in that way, but if they do they'll ask a question like, "What do you do outside of work". This question is about your work and career.

What they really want to know

This is one of the first questions asked, so at this point recruiters or hiring managers are just interested in knowing a few things. First, they want to get a feel for your ability to have a conversation, ie. can you give a clear, sensical answer and not drone on and on or say something strange. Don't worry about this- giving clear answers is easy and we'll show you how.

They also want to know that you've grown and progressed in your work life. Where have you shown initiative? How have you challenged yourself? Recruiters and hiring managers want to know that you can learn and make progress, which is something everyone has to do when they start a new role (particularly if they're breaking into the field of data).

How to answer

If this question seems daunting, don't worry- this is actually one of the easier questions to answer. Before we jump in, based on what you've read above, how would you answer this? Go ahead and take a minute and give your full response, out loud if you can.

Now let's go through some recommendations and start to formulate the perfect answer. Remember that, like everything else in this strategy guide, this information is based on our experience as both candidates and hiring managers, as well as information we've gathered by talking with candidates, hiring managers, and recruiters. We've had a lot of failures and a lot of success answering all of these questions, so rest assured that you're getting the full benefit of what we know.

First, before brainstorming how you want to answer a question, make a list of what you want to communicate. This is an incredibly helpful step that will help you create great responses and put you ahead of the pack. Here is an example from one candidate, interviewing from a Data Scientist role:

- I have done challenging and important work

- I have sought creative ways to solve problems

- I have challenged myself to build skills to solve those problems

If you were a hiring manager, how would you feel about hiring someone with these traits? Probably pretty great- these are great attributes for anyone in any role to possess. Think about what you want to communicate, but make it a relatively short list (3 items is usually enough).

Now, let's think about our response in light of the things we'd like to communicate, continuing to use the above as an example. For each item, write a sentence from your work or college history that applies. It can be specific, because you're going to be asked about projects and other details later.

- I have done challenging and important work

Example: I started at {Company} in a marketing role, first working on email campaigns and then gradually working on bigger and bigger projects.

- I have sought creative ways to solve problems

While in that role, I noticed that our work would get delayed if an analyst was out sick or if there was turnover, because we needed lots of data for marketing. I decided to take it upon myself to learn how to get that data.

- I have challenged myself to build skills to solve those problems

I taught myself SQL by taking online courses, reading books, and working with other analysts in the company. After getting comfortable there, I expanded into Python and started automating our workflows, which is saving us a lot of time.

Does that make sense? When you answer open-ended questions (any of them), you want to make no more than 2-3 clear, concise points, illustrated with examples. Now, let's string these together to form a complete answer:

Interviewer: "Why don't we start with you telling me a little bit about yourself?"

You: "Sure, no problem. I started at {Company} in a marketing role. It's been a great experience because I started with basic email campaigns, and gradually worked on bigger and bigger projects, even leading some of them. While in the role I noticed that our work would get delayed if an analyst was out sick or if there was turnover, because we needed lots of data for marketing. I decided to learn how to get the data myself by teaching myself SQL. I took online courses, read books, and collaborated with other analysts in the company. After getting comfortable with SQL, I expanded Python and am excited to say we're now automating many of our workflows, which is a huge time-saver."

Notice that the wording is a bit different than the individual points above- this is intentional. It is very important that you start with the points you want to communicate and really know those well, then practice giving complete answers. For this question and others, always start with what you want to communicate- start at a high level and fill in the details.

Where a lot of candidates mess up is when they'll do some research online for interview questions, write out their answers, and practice the answers verbatim- but they don't think about the points they're trying to communicate. When it comes time to actually be in an interview and answer the questions, their mind goes blank and they say maybe half their answer (and it's not very good). Has this ever happened to you? Thankfully you have this approach now and know what you need to do to be successful.

Tell me about your current role

You'll probably get asked this a few times- usually first by the recruiter in the initial phone screen. Be prepared to answer this question for any hiring manager interview, as well as any non-technical interviews you have with the company.

What they're really asking

"Tell me about your role" is one of the more transparent questions we'll cover in this chapter. Here, the hiring manager or recruiter does truly want to know about your current role, but there's one question you should ask yourself: if the recruiter or hiring manager has your resume, which has your current role and some bullet points you've included, so why would they ask you this?

Simple answer- they want more context. They want to hear how you think about and explain your job. Most candidates fluff up their resumes and descriptions, so the hiring team wants to hear about your work in your own words.

What they really want to know

First, they want to know that you can speak to your current role clearly. You need to be able to explain what you do in clear, precise language. This is a challenge for some people, especially those who wear many hats at work. They're often tempted to say something like, "Oh, I do a little bit of everything..." and then gloss over some of the basics of their work. Unfortunately, this is a poor strategy- it may seem counterintuitive but nobody wants to hire someone who, "does a little bit of everything". It's OK if you have a lot of responsibilities, but you want to be clear and emphasize the major parts of your role and the parts that apply to the role you're interviewing for.

They also want to know that you've done work that's important to your current company. Most questions are about the recruiter or hiring manager trying to understand your value, and one of the best proxies for how valuable you'll be to their company is how valuable you are to your current company. Do you manage people or lead important projects? Are you the go-to person in a certain area of expertise? These are all things that demonstrate high value, but even if you're not "the best" at anything in particular, you're still valuable. How do we know you're valuable?

Because your company pays you to be there. It doesn't matter if you're making cold calls or running a division or sweeping the floor- remember that you do have value and show the hiring team.

How to answer

The two main things you want to emphasize when answering this question are that you do valuable work at your current company, and the work you do is relevant to the role you're applying for. For most people the latter is tricky if they're trying to break into the field of data, but if understand what the new role is looking for and think about all the different parts of your current job, you should be able to find some similarities. Let's separate out our points and add some hypothetical context. For illustration we'll assume this is for a Data Scientist role, and the job description mentions user conversion analysis.

- The work I do is valuable to my current company.

I lead many of our marketing initiatives which are the primary way we acquire new customers. I focus on figuring out which programs are most effective and with this data I recommend strategies based on where I think our money is best spent.

- The work I do is relevant to the role I'm applying for.

In order to determine the most effective marketing efforts, I spend time analyzing and thinking about the conversion channel, particularly for email marketing. This involves looking at the number of emails we sent (minus the bounce rate), our open rate, our click through rate, and ultimately our conversion to a customer. This allows us to optimize each step of the funnel and produce really effective marketing campaigns.

This is all it really takes. The last section in this chapter will go over high-level tips, but by now you're getting the hang of it: figure out the 2-3 things you'd like to communicate, and do so with clear, concise statements that get to the point quickly. Don't overthink it. You don't have to explain everything in one go because you'll probably be asked follow-up questions.

What are you looking for in your next role?

This is another question you're likely to hear a few times, most likely by both the recruiter and hiring manager. The good news is that you can have pretty much the same response for both interviewers, since they're looking for the same things.

What they're really asking

They're really asking- does this person actually want to work in this role and at this company, and is it for good reasons? Good reasons are that you're looking for more challenge and growth, you're looking to work with best-in-class data teams, and/or that you love the company/product and are interested in tackling tricky problems. Bad reasons are that you're looking for better pay (yes, candidates say this) or something generic like "I'm looking to do more analytical work" (duh).

What they really want to know

The main thing the hiring team wants to know with this question is that you actually want to do the role you're applying for. It may sound crazy, but there are a lot of candidates who will apply to and interview for a role that has nothing to do with their aspirations or even work they're interested in.

For example, we've seen candidates apply for Business Analyst roles that are very straightforward analytics roles involving lots of SQL, Python, business strategy, dashboarding, etc. While these are great roles, sometimes when we ask candidates what they're looking for in their next role they respond with things like, "I'd love to work on Machine Learning problems, and I've been working on Neural Nets in my spare time so I'd love to tackle those sorts of projects." At that point we know it's pretty much a non-starter.

Thoughts from a Hiring Manager

"The last thing I want is to hire someone for a role they don't want because that is a recipe for dissatisfaction on both sides. Even if my team is really under the gun and we need someone ASAP, I just can't bring myself to hire someone as a Data Analyst if they really want to be an ML Engineer, or anything else that is a mismatch. I know that even if they say they want to do the role and have all the ability in the world, I know they won't be happy long-term if they're looking for a completely different role"

Let's be clear- it's OK to aspire to different and more challenging work. After all, most people need a few foundational roles (such as Data Analyst) if they want to eventually work up to harder technical problems or management. The question is asking what you're looking for in your next role, so articulate that clearly. State your 2-3 main points, and if you'd like it's OK to add something like, "Long-term I think I'd look to work into Machine Learning problems, and potentially Neural Nets". This, combined with your other answers, shows that you're looking to grow and contribute more to the next company you join.

How to answer

What are the main points we want to articulate? Your exact answers may vary, but let's dive right in using a Product Analyst role at Uber as an example.

- I'm excited about this role, specifically

I'm excited about the Product Analyst role because I've always enjoyed working with Product- both digging into current products and using data to think about the strategic direction of how we interact with consumers.

- I'm excited about this company, specifically

I'm interested in this opportunity specifically because I'm an avid Uber user, and I've always been interested in the different types of problems to solve. From things like Rider Wait Time to New Driver Acquisition, I feel like this is a role and company where I could both learn a lot and contribute the knowledge I've gained in my current role to help drive the product forward.

What do we notice? The answer is specific to both the company and the role, and demonstrates general enthusiasm for the work. We know that this person is truly interested in this opportunity and likely won't be looking to jump to a different job soon after they're hired. This answer is short and sweet, but still articulates enough information for the recruiter or hiring manager to feel good about their candidacy.

Tell me about one of your projects

This question is definitely more common in hiring manager interviews, but also pops up in recruiter interviews occasionally. Hiring managers like to ask follow-up questions for this one, so be prepared to speak to details about your work.

What they're really asking

Here the recruiter or hiring manager is really asking, "Tell me about one of your important projects that made a real contribution to the company." Again, they're asking about the relevance of your current work and the value you bring to the table. They're asking themselves, "Can this candidate do the work of the role I'm hiring for? Can they make meaningful contributions to this company without too much training and ramp-up?"

What they really want to know

The hiring team wants to know a few things. Number one, that you've worked on significant value-generating projects in your current role. They want to know that you're trusted with important work and can execute when it's time to produce results.

They also want to know that you can overcome challenges and barriers. Almost all projects have roadblocks, so don't hesitate to call those out and talk about how you navigated to a great outcome. This is your time to show that you will be effective with whatever they task you with. Bonus points if you illustrate how you collaborated with others and used your soft skills to help get things done- "I stayed up all night working on XYZ" is OK at best (but is probably detrimental)- show that you were able to work collaboratively with others to get the job done and they'll be impressed.

How to answer

Yet again, think about what you want to communicate that will generally align with what the recruiter or hiring manager wants to know about you when they ask this question. Put simply, you want to illustrate that you work on important value-adding projects to the company, and you also understand how to work through problems to achieve a positive outcome.

Additionally, since we're talking about a project, let's try incorporating something new. it's called the SCORE framework, and was originally introduced by McKinsey & Company, one of the top consulting firms in the world. SCORE stands for Situation, Conflict, Resolution (don't ask why they had to add the additional letters). Let's try an example:

Situation: Our email marketing campaigns are one of the top channels for for new customer acquisition, and last quarter we were getting ready for our biggest email push of the year.

Conflict: One of our major blockers for marketing campaigns would be when our marketing analyst was out sick, too busy, or otherwise couldn't help with list pulls or analyses.

Resolution: I anticipated that the analyst not being available to help and decided to take it into my own hands. Because I had a few months until the big email push, I started teaching myself SQL and really getting immersed in how we pull and analyze data by collaborating with other analysts. When it came time to launch the campaign, and later analyze it, I was actually able to handle all of the data needs myself and ensure that we could execute the launch without any delays. It ended up being our most successful marketing campaign in several years, and now we're set up to be a self-sufficient marketing team while still having other analytical resources when we need them.

This isn't the only way to answer the question, but we're bringing up the SCORE framework because most candidates struggle not because they haven't done relevant or important projects, but because they don't understand how to articulate the details of a project clearly. Many candidates either don't give enough information or get into the weeds and tell a long, winding story without much of a point. Clear, concise communication wins the day.

Why ___ company?

You could hear this question from anyone you interview with, and it's very prevalent in recruiter phone screens as well as cross-functional or fit/culture interviews. This should be one of the easier questions to answer, since you're at least somewhat interested in the company if you're interviewing.

What they're really asking

They're really asking, "Does this person actually want to work here, or do they just want a job? Do they even know what we do and/or are they a user of our product?". They're trying to get a sense of how you feel about the company, and how much you know about what they do.

What they want to know

It's important that recruiters and hiring managers know you're interested in the company itself, because they're going to spend a lot of time and money to train and ramp up whomever they hire, and they want to make sure that person is going to stick around. They don't want to hire someone who is looking for a stepping-stone job or someone who is going to get bored and leave in a year. They want someone who's in it for the long term, and part of that is a solid interest in the company.

They also want to know that you'll be happy if you get the job, and part of that is how much you like the company. If you feel that you work at a company with an amazing product and team, then it's a lot more likely that you'll be happy and stay happy. It's difficult to work with people who have no interest in the company because although many times they're competent and a good performer, they don't have much "juice" or energy to do really outstanding work. Just about every hiring manager would rather that a great data professional leave the company and go do something they really enjoy than have them stick around and be dissatisfied.

How to answer

This should be pretty simple, but maybe a different phrasing would be helpful. If you think about why you want to work at XYZ company, you initial thoughts may be that it's a great brand, or the role is a big step up, or even that you think the perks would be awesome. Those are absolutely

OK to think, but they probably won't help you answer this question effectively.

Try answering this question instead: what do you respect about XYZ company? If interviewing for a Data Scientist role within Google Maps, you might say, "Well I think it's a fantastic product, and it's my understanding that Google has the best data scientists in the world. I use Google Maps for everything from biking directions to restaurant recommendations, so I'd love to work on this product and tackle interesting problems. I'm interested in Google because it would be a great opportunity for me to both learn from some of the best minds in data and also contribute my talent to help the product grow."

It's a good exercise to think about how typical interview questions might be rephrased. There can be a lot of "whys" to why you want to work at a company, and there's nothing wrong with pay and perks playing a part. But when you think about what you genuinely respect about a company and can articulate that, it gets hiring teams excited to bring you on.

How to Implement the Master Plan

Now that we're done going through the top five questions, let's take a step back and think about how you should approach answering these and any other questions that come up. The candidates who do the best and ultimately get the best job offers almost always have a structured approach to answering interview questions.

    Before you even start to answer a question, ask yourself those two questions: what are they really asking, and what do they want to know? While it's true you won't know exactly what is on someone's mind, try to think generally. They want someone who adds value, will be good at the job, is interested in the role specifically, wants to work at the company specifically, etc. As you're using this chapter and researching more interview questions, think about these two questions first.

    Two things you need to keep in mind (write them down right now): Clear and Concise. You should strive to have everything you say or write to be clear and concise. Clear: is what I'm saying easy to understand? Am I getting my point across? Is it easy to figure out exactly what my point is? Concise: am I getting to the point quickly? Am I answering without a long-winded story? Am I using no more than 2-3 clear points? Most candidates focus only on what they're going to say, rather than how they're going to say it- clear and concise is a major tip that will put you far ahead of the pack.

On that note, part of your approach for brainstorming answers to interview questions should be to write out the 2-3 things you'd like to communicate. Never start by writing or typing a full-paragraph answer to the question. Ask yourself, "What do I want to say? What do I want to communicate?" Once you have your 2-3 points, add context relevant to the question (eg. about a project you've worked on). Then, string it all together to make a clear and concise answer. Don't go on forever, but you don't have to be super brief- say what you need to say.

Some final tips: smile during interviews, even if you're on the phone. People like to be around people who are happy and engaged, and it energizes them. Show that you're enthusiastic about the role and company. If you can't get excited in the interview stage, how will you feel when you're actually in the role? Don't go crazy, but don't be afraid to show that you're excited.

That's it for this chapter. We recommend reading through it once first, then giving it another detailed read when you're preparing for your interviews. The great part about the content we've given you is that the ideas and approach will easily transfer to other interview questions. Read this chapter, know what you want to communicate, and practice, and you'll be in great shape.

Expanded Questions

Alright, now it's your turn to go through the process. We've combed through our own data and research and are providing another 15 questions from real interviews- make sure these are in your repertoire.

Remember that there are three questions you need to ask yourself when preparing for a particular interview question: What are they really asking? What do they really want to know? How should I answer? In answering the last question, you'll also want to write down what you want to communicate, which should align with what they really want to know.

This approach is crucial for getting into the rhythm of answering interview questions because you're not going to be able to memorize all possible answers, and even if you could it wouldn't be a good idea. Let's get started.

What's important to you when you're looking at companies?

Do you understand how our business works?

How will this role take you to your goals?

Tell me about a time when you had to make a decision without all of the information

How do you deal with data skepticism from non-technical people?

How do you communicate with up-level stakeholders?

Why are you leaving your current company?

What is some feedback you've received, both positive and constructive?

Tell me about a time you failed

Tell me about a time you had to approach something in a structured way

Tell me about a time you weren't able to collaborate effectively with a cross-functional partner

What's your process for getting information out of a cross-functional partner?

What does your team do?

Explain a technical concept related to [role you're applying for]

How would you explain [XYZ concept] to a Product Manager without a technical background?

www.ingramcontent.com/pod-product-compliance
Lightning Source LLC
Chambersburg PA
CBHW030602220526
45463CB00007B/3147